Gratitude

A JOURNAL

CHRONICLE BOOKS
SAN FRANCISCO

ISBN 978-0-8118-6720-7

Manufactured in China
Design by Jennifer Tolo Pierce
Typeset in Chaparral Pro and Meta Plus
Chronicle Books endeavors to use
environmentally responsible paper in
its gift and stationery products.

20 19 18 17 16 15 14 13 12

Chronicle Books LLC
680 Second Street
San Francisco, CA 94107
www.chroniclebooks.com

INTRODUCTION

If you're anything like me, you probably spend more time thinking about your problems than you do reflecting on the good things in your life. It makes sense—problems need to be solved, whereas good things are, well, good. So of course the bad stuff winds up getting more of our attention.

For a long time, psychology took the same approach: Most research focused on how to alleviate people's suffering rather than on how to actively make us feel better. Psychologists assumed that we were each born with a "happiness set point"—a genetically determined level of happiness to which we were fated always to return—and there wasn't much we could do about it.

But now, that idea is changing. Research from the burgeoning field of positive psychology has suggested that while some of our happiness is indeed influenced by our genes and our external circumstances, a large part of it—up to 40 percent—might come from how we choose to approach our lives. In other words, there's plenty of wiggle room.

I personally experimented with this wiggle room a year or so ago, when I agreed to spend six weeks trying out a bunch of positive psychology exercises—the kinds advocated by researchers like Sonja Lyubomirsky, Martin E. Seligman, and Robert Emmons. I wrote lists of things that made me happy. I took quizzes to find out my "signature strengths" and tried to find ways to use them. I composed a letter to my grandmother telling her how much I loved her and what an influence she'd had on my life. I wanted to see if a month and a half of "overdosing on joy" would make me feel happier.

While trying out these exercises, I noticed that one theme tied them together: gratitude. Whether I was consciously trying to notice moments of beauty in my day or doing a favor for a stranger, everything seemed to come back to the idea of appreciating the things, experiences, and people around me. This idea of thankfulness seems simple, but researchers have found it to be surprisingly powerful: People who actively try to become more grateful in their everyday lives are happier—not to mention healthier—than those who don't.

That's where this journal comes in. Filled with quotations, exercises, and writing prompts, it's designed to help you keep your happiness at the front of your mind—and to prevent your journal from devolving, as often ends up happening, into to-do lists or detailed descriptions of things in your life that are stressing you out. At its most basic level, this is simply a "gratitude journal"—a place to keep track of things in your life that you're grateful for. But there are all sorts of other happiness- and mindfulness-inducing exercises for you to try.

Before you start this journal, there are a few basic things to keep in mind. First, stick with it! Learning to refocus your mind toward happiness is a long process and can have its frustrations as well as its joys. Think of your journaling as being like exercise—it'll take a while to get yourself "in shape," and even once you've gotten into a routine, there will still be days when you just don't feel like writing anything. That's okay.

It's also important to remember that this journal and its exercises should never leave you feeling guilty. No one is happy all the time, and for me at least, trying to think about things to be happy about when I am in a bad mood only makes me crankier. If the only thing you want to do with this journal is hurl it at a passerby, try this technique I cribbed from meditation teacher James Baraz: Take a few deep breaths and try to identify how your mind and body are actually feeling. Are you stressed? Angry? Frightened? Anxious? Without putting a story on it (e.g. Don't say, "I'm angry at my boss for making that comment in the meeting today—why is she always putting me down in front of my professional peers? I hate her so much!"), try to just allow yourself to experience the actual sensations in your body and to give the feeling itself a name. As you continue to take deep breaths, spend five minutes or so writing about how this emotion resonates in your body. If this makes you feel better, great. If not, don't beat yourself up. Sometimes, we just have bad days.

The same is true for times when you're suffering. If you or a family member just received bad news, or if a loved one has died, don't try to force yourself to adopt a Pollyanna attitude. Allow yourself to experience whatever emotions have surfaced. At the same time, if you find yourself having joyful moments even in the midst of your grief, don't feel guilty about it! The worse things are, the more important it is to appreciate the moments in your life that feel good.

Also, while most of these exercises can be mixed and matched, depending on what you feel like writing about each day, there are a few guidelines to keep in mind: Researchers suggest limiting your gratitude lists (lists of things you're grateful for) to once a week—one study found that writing one list a week actually had a much stronger effect on people's moods than doing so three times a week. Restricting yourself will help the exercise stay fresh.

If you want something to do every day, though, follow the prompts included throughout the journal, or try the "three blessings" approach endorsed by positive psychologists like Martin Seligman and Chris Peterson: Write down three things in your day that went well—and then jot down a few sentences on *why* these things happened. They don't have to be big—something as simple as "my daughter cleaned her room today" could suffice. But the act of reflecting on why this happened (e.g. "because I have encouraged her to feel a sense of pride and ownership over her belongings") can help identify habits that lead to good outcomes. We spend an awful lot of time analyzing things that go wrong in our lives—why not devote equal thought to what goes right?

Lastly, whenever people write about happiness, they come up against the inevitable question of how happiness is actually defined. For the purposes of this journal, we're using a conception of happiness favored by people like Martin Seligman—it's about feeling good in the moment, sure, but also about developing a meaningful life in which you feel actively engaged.

As for my own experiment: At the end of the six weeks, I felt a definite improvement. I hadn't developed into some insufferably upbeat person who encouraged friends to turn their frowns upside down. Rather, I felt something deeper inside me begin to change: I was training myself to appreciate the everyday beauty and joy that already existed in my life, and I was beginning to understand how I could create more of those experiences. It was surprisingly empowering—and definitely worth the effort. The most heartening part? My experiment only lasted six weeks. Imagine what might happen if you did it for a whole year.

RECOMMENDED READING ON GRATITUDE AND HAPPINESS

Csikszentmihalyi, Mihaly. *Flow: The Psychology of Optimal Experience*. New York: HarperPerennial, 1991.

Emmons, Robert. *Thanks! How the New Science of Gratitude Can Make You Happier*. New York: Houghton Mifflin, 2007.

Foster, Rick and Greg Hicks. *How We Choose to Be Happy: The 9 Choices of Extremely Happy People—Their Secrets, Their Stories*. New York: Perigee Trade, 2004.

Lyubomirsky, Sonja. *The How of Happiness: A Scientific Approach to Getting the Life You Want*. New York: Penguin Press, 2007.

McCullough, Michael. *Beyond Revenge: The Evolution of the Forgiveness Instinct*. San Francisco: Jossey-Bass, 2008.

Peterson, Christopher. *A Primer in Positive Psychology*. New York: Oxford University Press, 2006.

Ratey, John J. and Eric Hagerman. *Spark: The Revolutionary New Science of Exercise and the Brain.* New York: Little, Brown and Company, 2008.

Seligman, Martin E. *Authentic Happiness: Using the New Positive Psychology to Realize Your Potential for Lasting Fulfillment.* New York: Free Press, 2004.

Seligman, Martin E. *Learned Optimism: How to Change Your Mind and Your Life.* New York: Vintage, 2006.

Weiner, Eric. *The Geography of Bliss: One Grump's Search for the Happiest Places in the World.* New York: Twelve, 2008.

OTHER RESOURCES

James Baraz's "Awakening Joy" online class offers a 10-month interactive course geared toward increasing your happiness. For more info, visit www.awakeningjoy.info

PICK OUT THREE THINGS IN YOUR DAY THAT ARE BEAUTIFUL.
Take time to notice and appreciate them in the moment; then,
when you get home, jot them down in your journal.

Let us be grateful to people who make us happy; they are the charming gardeners who make our souls blossom.

MARCEL PROUST (1871–1922), French novelist

SAVOR SOMETHING — stay in the shower for an extra few seconds, or take a moment to appreciate the smell of your morning coffee before your first sip. Try to elongate the pleasant moments of your day, no matter how small.

GRATITUDE LIST: Write a list of things in your life you're grateful for.

> *To learn from our enemies is the best pathway to loving them: for it makes us grateful to them.*

FRIEDRICH NIETZSCHE (1844–1900), German philosopher, classical scholar, critic of culture

---

 THREE GOOD THINGS: Write down three things that went well in your day and *why* they went well. These don't have to be big events—you're simply trying to train your mind to dwell more on the positive. For example: "The barista at the coffee shop remembered my drink without asking what I wanted." (Reason: "Because I try to be friendly and have gotten to know the staff.") Figuring out the reason good things happen—whether or not you yourself are responsible for them—can help make you more prone to appreciate good things and deeds when they occur.

- -

- -

- -

- -

- -

- -

- -

- -

- -

- -

- -

- -

- -

 TAKE A FEW MINUTES TO WRITE DOWN WHY YOU'VE DECIDED TO KEEP THIS JOURNAL. What are you hoping to accomplish? What are your personal intentions for it? Throughout the year, keep flipping back to this page to keep yourself on track.

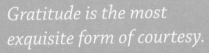

Gratitude is the most exquisite form of courtesy.

JACQUES MARITAIN (1882–1973), French philosopher

TAKE A "MUSIC BATH"—find a comfortable spot to relax in, pick out a favorite song or piece of music, turn off the lights, close your eyes, and *listen.* (You want the music to be loud enough that it envelops you, but not so loud that it hurts your ears.)

- -

- -

- -

- -

- -

- -

- -

- -

- -

- -

- -

- -

- -

- -

- -

- -

- -

THREE GOOD THINGS: Write down three things that went well in your day and *why* they went well.

CREATE A LIST OF ACTIVITIES THAT MAKE YOU HAPPY.
Then put a check mark next to the ones that you do on a
regular basis. Is there a way you could incorporate these more
frequently into your daily life? This week, try to do at least
three activities on your list. Write about the experience.

"

Thanksgiving comes to us out of the prehistoric dimness, universal to all ages and all faiths. At whatever straws we must grasp, there is always a time for gratitude and new beginnings.

J. ROBERT MOSKIN (1923–), author and
World War II veteran

"

THREE GOOD THINGS: Write down three things that went well in your day and *why* they went well.

START THE PROCESS OF WRITING A GRATITUDE LETTER.
Make a list of important people in your life who have made
a major positive difference and whom you've never fully
thanked. You'll write the actual letters later—for now, just
get down the list of people and write brief notes on what
impact each person has had on your life.

DATE ___ / ___ / ___

SET ASIDE SEVERAL QUIET MINUTES TODAY and do something that you find nourishing, like meditating, taking a walk, or having a cup of tea.

> *Gratitude among friends is like credit among tradesmen: it keeps business up, and maintains commerce. And we pay not because it is just to discharge our debts, but that we might the more easily find lenders on another occasion.*

FRANÇOIS, DUC DE LA ROCHEFOUCAULD (1613–1680),
French writer, moralist

_____

- -

- -

- -

- -

- -

- -

- -

- -

- -

- -

- -

- -

- -

- -

- -

- -

THREE GOOD THINGS: Write down three things that went well in your day and *why* they went well.

GRATITUDE LIST: Write a list of things in your life that you're grateful for.

 PUT ON SOME MUSIC AND SING ALONG. If that's not your thing, write, draw, or dance—or indulge in some other sort of creative outlet that you enjoy.

THREE GOOD THINGS: Write down three things that went well in your day and *why* they went well.

- -

- -

- -

- -

- -

- -

- -

- -

- -

- -

- -

- -

- -

CONTINUE THE STEPS TOWARD YOUR GRATITUDE LETTER.
From the list you made several pages back, choose one person
to whom you'll write, and start drafting the letter by noting
down what you'd like to thank him or her for. Be specific and
concrete: What did he or she do, and how does that still affect
your life?

WHAT DOES THE WORD GRATITUDE MEAN TO YOU?
Describe a situation when you have felt especially grateful.

No one is as capable of grati-
tude as one who has emerged
from the kingdom of night.

ELIE WIESEL (1928–), writer, political activist,
Holocaust survivor, Nobel laureate

THREE GOOD THINGS: Write down three things that went well in your day and *why* they went well.

MOVE YOUR BODY AT LEAST 2 TO 3 TIMES THIS WEEK. Run, bike, do yoga, dance, take a walk with a friend—anything that will get your heart pumping and blood moving. In addition to being good for your body, exercise also has a positive effect on your mind.

THREE GOOD THINGS: Write down three things that went well in your day and *why* they went well.

 FINISH YOUR GRATITUDE LETTER. Now, arrange a date to meet the recipient face-to-face (this exercise is more effective done in person)—but don't say why. Read the letter aloud to him or her and, after you're done, talk about the content of your letter and how you both feel about one another. (Bring tissues.) Afterward, write about the reaction and how it affected you, along with what it was like to write the letter in the first place. Don't be surprised if "happy" is not the first word that comes to mind—writing a gratitude letter can be an emotionally intense and somewhat exhausting process—but it's also often incredibly meaningful and rewarding for both people.

*Gratitude is a fruit of
great cultivation.*

SAMUEL JOHNSON (1709–1784), British writer, critic

GRATITUDE LIST: Write a list of things in your life that you're grateful for.

THINK OF A MOMENT IN YOUR LIFE WHEN YOU WERE COMPLETELY HAPPY AND WRITE ABOUT HOW IT FELT. What were you doing? How did the situation come to be? How did you feel (both emotionally and physically)? Was the physical sensation concentrated in a particular area of your body?

THREE GOOD THINGS: Write down three things that went well in your day and *why* they went well.

"

*A man's indebtedness . . .
is not virtue; his repayment
is. Virtue begins when he
dedicates himself actively to
the job of gratitude.*

RUTH BENEDICT (1887–1948), American anthropologist

"

- -

- -

- -

- -

- -

- -

- -

- -

- -

- -

- -

- -

- -

- -

- -

DESCRIBE A SITUATION when someone felt especially grateful toward you. Write about how that made you feel.

"

One of life's gifts is that each of us, no matter how tired and downtrodden, finds reasons for thankfulness: for the crops carried in from the fields and the grapes from the vineyard.

J. ROBERT MOSKIN (1923–), author and World War II veteran

"

THREE GOOD THINGS: Write down three things that went well in your day and *why* they went well.

TODAY, TRY TO PAY ATTENTION TO SOMETHING YOU DON'T NORMALLY PUT ANY THOUGHT INTO—or even something you don't usually enjoy, like washing dishes or chopping vegetables or sitting in traffic. Try to find something in the experience that is enjoyable or beautiful, or both. Write about the experience.

MOVE YOUR BODY AT LEAST 2 TO 3 TIMES THIS WEEK. Run, bike, do yoga, dance, take a walk with a friend—anything that will get your heart pumping and blood moving. In addition to being good for your body, exercise also has a positive effect on your mind.

 TAKE A MENTAL SCAN OF YOUR BODY, MAKING A NOTE OF ANY AREAS THAT FEEL TIGHT OR TENSE. Then take 10 slow, deep breaths through your nose. Try imagining that you're inhaling air straight to the top of your head and exhaling a sense of relaxation down through the rest of your body, concentrating on the areas that feel the most tense.

THREE GOOD THINGS: Write down three things that went well in your day and *why* they went well.

GRATITUDE LIST: Write a list of things in your life that you're grateful for. (If you find yourself always listing the same things, pick different contexts to focus on: things about your family, things at work, things in the external world, et cetera.)

You never really appreciate a thing until you have to give it up.

JOHN RHODES STURDY (1911–), Canadian screenwriter

- -

- -

- -

- -

- -

- -

- -

- -

- -

- -

- -

- -

- -

- -

- -

THREE GOOD THINGS: Write down three things that went well in your day and *why* they went well.

It takes patience to appreciate
domestic bliss; volatile spirits
prefer unhappiness.

GEORGE SANTAYANA (1863–1952),
American philosopher, poet

DRAFT ANOTHER GRATITUDE LETTER. From the original list of recipients, choose one person to whom you'll write, and start the letter by noting down what you'd like to thank him or her for. Be specific and concrete: What did he or she do, and how does that still affect your life?

WRITE DOWN THREE THINGS IN YOUR DAILY LIFE THAT YOU TAKE FOR GRANTED. For example: your dog, your sense of balance, the fact that you have hot water for your shower.

THREE GOOD THINGS: Write down three things that went well in your day and *why* they went well.

> *In the midst of happiness,*
> *one may not appreciate what*
> *happiness is.*
>
> CHINESE PROVERB

MOVE YOUR BODY AT LEAST 2 TO 3 TIMES THIS WEEK. Run, bike, do yoga, dance, take a walk with a friend—anything that will get your heart pumping and blood moving. In addition to being good for your body, exercise also has a positive effect on your mind.

DATE   /   /

 WHEN SOMETHING POSITIVE HAPPENS TODAY, take note of what the experience does to your body. What does it mean to actually *feel* happy? How does it affect how you breathe and move?

THREE GOOD THINGS: Write down three things that went well in your day and *why* they went well.

To give thanks in solitude is enough. Thanksgiving has wings and goes where it must go. Your prayer knows much more about it than you do.

VICTOR HUGO (1802–1885), French poet, novelist, playwright, essayist

- -

- -

- -

- -

- -

- -

- -

- -

- -

- -

- -

- -

- -

- -

- -

- -

- -

GRATITUDE LIST: Write a list of things in your life that you're grateful for.

 WHAT DID YOU ENJOY TODAY? Write about it.

_____

- -

- -

- -

- -

- -

- -

- -

- -

- -

- -

- -

- -

- -

- -

- -

- -

- -

THREE GOOD THINGS: Write down three things that went well in your day and *why* they went well.

> *Without having experienced the cold of winter, one cannot appreciate the warmth of spring.*
>
> CHINESE PROVERB

- -

- -

- -

- -

- -

- -

- -

- -

- -

- -

- -

- -

- -

- -

- -

BEFORE YOU EAT ONE OF YOUR MEALS TODAY, take a moment to think about where your food actually came from, and give thanks to whatever part of the process you feel the most resonance with.

DATE   /   /

THREE GOOD THINGS: Write down three things that went well in your day and *why* they went well.

FINISH YOUR GRATITUDE LETTER. Now, arrange a date to meet the recipient face-to-face—but don't say why. Read the letter aloud to him or her, and after you're done, talk about the content of your letter and how you both feel about one another. (Again, don't forget the tissues.) Afterward, write about the reaction and how it affected you, along with what it was like to write the letter in the first place.

When a noble deed is done,
who is likely to appreciate it?
They who are noble themselves.

HENRY DAVID THOREAU (1817–1862), American
philosopher, author, naturalist

MOVE YOUR BODY AT LEAST 2 TO 3 TIMES THIS WEEK. Run, bike, do yoga, dance, take a walk with a friend—anything that will get your heart pumping and blood moving. In addition to being good for your body, exercise also has a positive effect on your mind.

 GRATITUDE LIST: Write a list of things in your life that you're grateful for. (Remember, if you find yourself always listing the same things, pick different contexts to focus on: things about your family, things at work, things in the external world, et cetera.)

THREE GOOD THINGS: Write down three things that went well in your day and *why* they went well.

TODAY, DURING YOUR FAVORITE MEAL, slow down as you
eat your first bite, allowing yourself to appreciate the texture
and flavor of the food. How does slowing down change
the experience?

> To appreciate heaven well
> 'Tis good for a man to have
> some fifteen minutes of hell.

WILL CARLETON (1845–1912), American poet

THREE GOOD THINGS: Write down three things that went well in your day and *why* they went well.

TAKE A MINDFUL WALK AROUND YOUR NEIGHBORHOOD.
Try to notice details that usually pass you by: What color
is your neighbor's house? What species of trees line your
blocks? Is anything new in bloom?

> *Happiness lies neither in vice nor in virtue; but in the manner we appreciate the one and the other, and the choice we make pursuant to our individual organization.*
>
> MARQUIS DE SADE (1740–1814), French author

THREE GOOD THINGS: Write down three things that went well in your day and *why* they went well.

 FOR HALF AN HOUR TODAY, UNITASK — do just one thing at a time, with no distractions or interruptions. How was the experience different from how you usually do things?

GRATITUDE LIST: Write a list of things in your life that you're grateful for.

- -

- -

- -

- -

- -

- -

- -

- -

- -

- -

- -

- -

- -

MOVE YOUR BODY AT LEAST 2 TO 3 TIMES THIS WEEK. Run, bike, do yoga, dance, take a walk with a friend—anything that will get your heart pumping and blood moving. In addition to being good for your body, exercise also has a positive effect on your mind.

"

Every day you must arise and say to your heart, "I have suffered enough and now I must live because the light of the sun must not be wasted, it must not be lost without an eye to appreciate it."

SIMONE SCHWARZ-BART (1938–), Guadeloupean author

"

THREE GOOD THINGS: Write down three things that went well in your day and *why* they went well.

TODAY, WHENEVER THE PHONE RINGS, YOUR COMPUTER IS BEING SLOW, OR YOU'RE WAITING IN LINE, take several deep, mindful breaths, allowing yourself to feel what it's like to fully inhale. As you exhale, try to relax your body. Pay attention to the sensations this evokes.

It is a conquest when we can lift ourselves above the annoyances of circumstances over which we have no control; but it is a greater victory when we can make those circumstances our helpers, when we can appreciate the good there is in them. It has often seemed to me as if Life stood beside me, looking me in the face, and saying, "Child, you must learn to like me in the form in which you see me, before I can offer myself to you in any other aspect."

LUCY LARCOM (1824–1893), American poet, teacher

DON'T TRY TO FORCE YOURSELF TO BE HAPPY. Everyone has bad days.

- -

- -

- -

- -

- -

- -

- -

- -

- -

- -

- -

- -

- -

- -

- -

- -

THREE GOOD THINGS: Write down three things that went well in your day and *why* they went well.

"

Objects are concealed from our view, not so much because they are out of the course of our visual ray as because we do not bring our minds and eyes to bear on them . . . there is just as much beauty visible to us in the landscape as we are prepared to appreciate— not a grain more.

HENRY DAVID THOREAU (1817–1862), American philosopher, author, naturalist

"

 WRITE ABOUT SOMETHING THAT HAPPENED IN YOUR DAY THAT LEFT YOU FEELING SATISFIED. What part did you play in achieving that sense of satisfaction?

DATE   /   /

- -

- -

- -

- -

- -

- -

- -

- -

- -

- -

- -

- -

- -

- -

- -

- -

THREE GOOD THINGS: Write down three things that went well in your day and *why* they went well.

The whole life of man is but a point of time; let us enjoy it, therefore, while it lasts, and not spend it to no purpose.

PLUTARCH (CIRCA 46 A.D.–119 A.D.),
Greek historian, writer

MOVE YOUR BODY AT LEAST 2 TO 3 TIMES THIS WEEK. Run, bike, do yoga, dance, take a walk with a friend—anything that will get your heart pumping and blood moving. In addition to being good for your body, exercise also has a positive effect on your mind.

TRY TO FIND A WAY TO MAKE A MUNDANE ACT MORE ENJOYABLE. If you're stuck in traffic, can you find a favorite song on the radio? Can you listen to a new podcast while tidying up your living space?

GRATITUDE LIST: Write a list of things in your life that you're grateful for.

DATE / /

THREE GOOD THINGS: Write down three things that went well in your day and *why* they went well.

*Gratitude is the sign of
noble souls.*

AESOP (620 B.C–560 B.C.), Greek slave, writer

WRITE ABOUT AN ASPECT OF YOUR BODY OR PERSONALITY THAT YOU DON'T LIKE. Then imagine you're your own best friend and write a counterargument in your own defense. In doing so, try to find a way to forgive yourself for whatever you beat yourself up for. To finish, write down several aspects of your body or your personality that you are grateful for, and explain why.

Gratitude is not only the greatest of virtues, but the parent of all the others.

MARCUS TULLIUS CICERO (106 B.C.–43 B.C.),
Roman statesman, writer, orator

THREE GOOD THINGS: Write down three things that went well in your day and *why* they went well.

- -

- -

- -

- -

- -

- -

- -

- -

- -

- -

- -

- -

- -

TAKE A MOMENT TO CHECK IN WITH YOURSELF. How are you feeling right now? Tired? Sad? Content? Stressed? Relaxed? Wherever you are is fine—just allow yourself to fully experience what the emotion feels like. Write about it. Then, if your current feeling is negative, see if you can imagine what it would be like to be in a more positive space. Write about it. See if the act of writing has an effect on your mood.

Gratitude is when memory is stored in the heart and not in the mind.

LIONEL HAMPTON (1908–2002), American jazz musician

DRAFT ANOTHER GRATITUDE LETTER. From the original list of recipients, choose one person to whom you'll write, and start drafting the letter by noting down what you'd like to thank him or her for. Be specific and concrete: What did he or she do, and how does that still affect your life?

MOVE YOUR BODY AT LEAST 2 TO 3 TIMES THIS WEEK. Run, bike, do yoga, dance, take a walk with a friend—anything that will get your heart pumping and blood moving. In addition to being good for your body, exercise also has a positive effect on your mind.

THREE GOOD THINGS: Write down three things that went well in your day and *why* they went well.

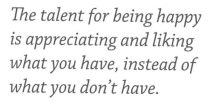

The talent for being happy is appreciating and liking what you have, instead of what you don't have.

WOODY ALLEN (1935–), American filmmaker

TAKE THREE TO FIVE MINUTES to write down everything you can think about to appreciate in this moment, right now, wherever you are. How does it feel, physically and emotionally, to pay attention to these things?

GRATITUDE LIST: Write a list of things in your life that you're grateful for.

THREE GOOD THINGS: Write down three things that went well in your day and *why* they went well.

> *If you concentrate on finding whatever is good in every situation, you will discover that your life will suddenly be filled with gratitude, a feeling that nurtures the soul.*
>
> HAROLD KUSHNER (1935–), American rabbi

DATE   /   /

 WHAT ARE YOU GRATEFUL FOR TODAY? Write about it.

TRY TO NOTICE SEVERAL POSITIVE MOMENTS IN YOUR DAY,
even if incidental—you found a parking spot in a crowded
neighborhood, you shared a joke with a coworker, a stranger
on the bus smiled at you. Write a brief description of what
these moments were and how they made you feel.

THREE GOOD THINGS: Write down three things that went well in your day and *why* they went well.

> *Happiness is not achieved by the conscious pursuit of happiness; it is generally the by-product of other activities.*
>
> ALDOUS HUXLEY (1894–1963), British writer

_____

- -

- -

- -

- -

- -

- -

- -

- -

- -

- -

- -

- -

- -

MOVE YOUR BODY AT LEAST 2 TO 3 TIMES THIS WEEK. Run, bike, do yoga, dance, take a walk with a friend—anything that will get your heart pumping and blood moving. In addition to being good for your body, exercise also has a positive effect on your mind.

 ASK YOURSELF WHAT WOULD MAKE YOU HAPPY RIGHT NOW.
If you can, do it.

THREE GOOD THINGS: Write down three things that went well in your day and *why* they went well.

 FINISH YOUR GRATITUDE LETTER. Now, arrange a date to meet the recipient face-to-face—but don't say why. Read the letter aloud to him or her, and after you're done, talk about the content of your letter and how you both feel about one another. (Again, don't forget the tissues.) Afterward, write about the reaction and how it affected you, along with what it was like to write the letter in the first place.

"

Gratitude bestows many benefits. It dissolves negative feelings: anger and jealousy melt in its embrace, fear and defensiveness shrink. Gratitude deflates the barriers to love.

ROGER WALSH (1946–), American psychiatrist, philosopher

"

THREE GOOD THINGS: Write down three things that went well in your day and *why* they went well.

 DESCRIBE WHAT IT WOULD TAKE for you to be truly happy in your life—and list the steps it would take to make that vision a reality. Is your vision realistic? If so, what is holding you back?

GRATITUDE LIST: Write a list of things in your life that you're grateful for.

> If the only prayer you ever say in your life is 'Thank you,' it will be enough.

MEISTER ECKHART (1260–1327), German theologian and philosopher

----

REESTABLISH CONTACT WITH AN OLD FRIEND.

THREE GOOD THINGS: Write down three things that went well in your day and *why* they went well.

TODAY, TRY SOMETHING THAT WILL GET YOU OUT OF YOUR USUAL ROUTINE — take a different route to work, eat something different for lunch, do a different type of exercise, sign up for a new class.

MOVE YOUR BODY AT LEAST 2 TO 3 TIMES THIS WEEK. Run, bike, do yoga, dance, take a walk with a friend—anything that will get your heart pumping and blood moving. In addition to being good for your body, exercise also has a positive effect on your mind.

 WRITE ABOUT A TIME IN THE PAST MONTH when you experienced great joy or well-being (or were filled with an intense sense of gratitude).

> *Happy is the man who can count his sufferings.*
>
> OVID (43 B.C.–17 A.D.), Roman poet

THREE GOOD THINGS: Write down three things that went well in your day and *why* they went well.

- -

- -

- -

- -

- -

- -

- -

- -

- -

- -

- -

- -

- -

- -

WRITE A LIST OF SIMPLE PLEASURES IN YOUR LIFE—
inconsequential, everyday things that make you happy, like
the smell of dryer sheets or the feeling of your cat brushing
against your leg.

"

A single thankful thought towards heaven is the most perfect of all prayers.

GOTTHOLD EPHRAIM LESSING (1729–1881),
German dramatist, critic

"

GRATITUDE LIST: Write a list of things in your life that you're grateful for.

DATE   /   /

THREE GOOD THINGS: Write down three things that went well in your day and *why* they went well.

- -

- -

- -

- -

- -

- -

- -

- -

- -

- -

- -

- -

- -

- -

- -

COMPLIMENT A STRANGER. Notice his or her response.

DATE / /

- -
- -
- -
- -
- -
- -
- -
- -
- -
- -
- -

THIS EXERCISE IS ADAPTED FROM *How We Choose to Be Happy* by Rick Foster and Greg Hicks: Write down a list of your most important long-term intentions. (For example, I intend to be a supportive parent. I intend to be a loving husband.) Evaluate your list. Get rid of those you feel you *should* do (as opposed to those you *want* to do). At the end of each, write "and I intend to be happy doing it." Do these feel authentic to you? Do they match what you've actually been doing in your life?

THREE GOOD THINGS: Write down three things that went well in your day and *why* they went well.

> *In this world of sin and sorrow there is always something to be thankful for.*
>
> H.L. (HENRY LEWIS) MENCKEN (1880–1956),
> American journalist, critic

DATE   /   /

 GO OUT OF YOUR WAY TO THANK SOMEONE TODAY.

WRITE DOWN THREE BLESSINGS—three things in your day
that went well for which you weren't personally responsible.

 MOVE YOUR BODY AT LEAST 2 TO 3 TIMES THIS WEEK. Run, bike, do yoga, dance, take a walk with a friend—anything that will get your heart pumping and blood moving. In addition to being good for your body, exercise also has a positive effect on your mind.

" "

Most human beings have an almost infinite capacity for taking things for granted.

ALDOUS HUXLEY (1894–1963), British writer

DATE   /   /

_____

DESCRIBE ONE OF THE HAPPIEST DAYS IN YOUR LIFE.
Who was involved? Is there a way you could thank them?

THREE GOOD THINGS: Write down three things that went well in your day and *why* they went well.

*O Lord, that lends me life,
lend me a heart replete with
thankfulness.*

WILLIAM SHAKESPEARE (1564–1616),
British poet, playwright

- -

- -

- -

- -

- -

- -

- -

- -

- -

- -

- -

- -

- -

- -

- -

- -

GRATITUDE LIST: Write a list of things in your life that you're grateful for.

DO SOMETHING NICE FOR SOMEONE ELSE TODAY — do a favor
for a friend, bring your coworker coffee, fold the laundry for
your partner without being asked.

If a man had no more to do with God than to be thankful, that would suffice.

MEISTER ECKHART (CIRCA 1260–1327),
German theologian, philosopher, mystic

THREE GOOD THINGS: Write down three things that went well in your day and *why* they went well.

 PLANT A PLEASANT SURPRISE FOR SOMEONE IN YOUR LIFE—get your officemate flowers, or present your partner with breakfast in bed.

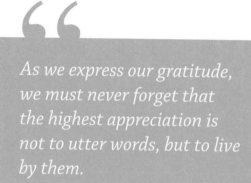

As we express our gratitude, we must never forget that the highest appreciation is not to utter words, but to live by them.

JOHN F. KENNEDY (1917–1963), American president

- -

- -

- -

- -

- -

- -

- -

- -

- -

- -

- -

- -

- -

- -

- -

- -

- -

THREE GOOD THINGS: Write down three things that went well in your day and *why* they went well.

MOVE YOUR BODY AT LEAST 2 TO 3 TIMES THIS WEEK. Run, bike, do yoga, dance, take a walk with a friend—anything that will get your heart pumping and blood moving. In addition to being good for your body, exercise also has a positive effect on your mind.

BUY A PIECE OF FOOD THAT YOU REALLY LOVE—a perfect orange, a fresh-baked cookie—and savor it with all your senses. What does it taste and look like? How does it smell? How does it feel in your hand, and what's the sound when you bite into it? See if you can do this for 10 minutes before you finish it. What did you notice that you haven't paid attention to before? What did you enjoy?

*You say grace before meals.
All right. But I say grace before
the concert and the opera,
and grace before the play and
pantomime, and grace before
I open a book, and grace before
sketching, painting, swimming,
fencing, boxing, walking, play-
ing, dancing, and grace before
I dip the pen in the ink.*

GILBERT KEITH CHESTERTON (1874–1936),
British writer

REREAD A FAVORITE POEM OR LETTER or a section of one of your most-loved books. Write down an excerpt.

DATE / /

 SET ASIDE A DAY THIS MONTH TO INDULGE IN YOUR FAVORITE PLEASURES—pamper yourself. Write down a detailed list of what you plan to do, hour by hour, and then do it.

GRATITUDE LIST: Write a list of things in your life that you're grateful for.

THREE GOOD THINGS: Write down three things that went well in your day and *why* they went well.

CARRY A CAMERA WITH YOU FOR A DAY and take photos of things you find beautiful or touching, or even just mundane things that make you happy. Write captions for your favorite shots, making sure to explain why you thought the subjects were picture-worthy.

> *The best remedy for those who are afraid, lonely or unhappy is to go outside, somewhere where they can be quiet, alone with the heavens, nature and God. Because only then does one feel that all is as it should be and that God wishes to see people happy, amidst the simple beauty of nature.*

ANNE FRANK (1929–1945), Holocaust victim, diarist

THREE GOOD THINGS: Write down three things that went well in your day and *why* they went well.

THIS EXERCISE IS EXCERPTED FROM *How We Choose to Be Happy* by Rick Foster and Greg Hicks: Ask yourself how you feel physically right at this moment. Then spend five minutes writing a list of everything that makes you happy, as quickly as possible. See how you feel. Are you surprised by what you wrote? Frustrated? Was it easy? Hard? How much of what you wrote is genuinely you, and how much is what you think you should enjoy?

- -

- -

- -

- -

- -

- -

- -

- -

- -

- -

GO TO PSYCHOLOGIST MARTIN SELIGMAN'S WEB SITE,
www.authentichappiness.org, and take a test of your
"signature strengths." Try to do several things this week
that highlight some of your top strengths—if you're
very generous and caring, for example, make a point of
volunteering or doing something for a friend. If your top
strength is "zest," sign up for something you've never
done before. Write about the experience and what effect
it has on your mood.

 FOR ONE DAY, TRY TO BASE YOUR DECISIONS ON WHAT WOULD MAKE YOU HAPPIEST in that particular moment. Are there situations when you could make this into a habit?

 LOOK BACK AT YOUR LIST OF THINGS IN YOUR LIFE that make you happy. Can you identify any themes? Are there any activities that would be easy to incorporate into your life that you're not currently doing? What's stopping you?

WRITE (AND SEND) A THANK-YOU NOTE TO SOMEONE—
for a gift, a favor, a good piece of advice—anything you feel
grateful for.

THREE GOOD THINGS: Write down three things that went well in your day and *why* they went well.

PICK OUT THREE THINGS IN YOUR DAY THAT ARE BEAUTIFUL.
Take time to notice and appreciate them in the moment; then,
when you get home, jot them down in your journal.

"

Gratitude to gratitude
always gives birth.

SOPHOCLES (497 B.C.–406/5 B.C.), Greek tragedian

"

THREE GOOD THINGS: Write down three things that went well in your day and *why* they went well.

 SET ASIDE SEVERAL QUIET MINUTES TODAY and do something that you find nourishing, like meditating, taking a walk, or having a cup of tea.

GRATITUDE LIST: Write a list of things in your life that you're grateful for.

DATE   /   /

WHAT DID YOU ENJOY TODAY? Write about it.

LOOK BACK OVER THIS JOURNAL AND REFLECT ON WHAT EFFECT KEEPING IT HAS HAD ON YOUR LIFE. What are some of your favorite exercises? Why do you think they were so effective? According to researchers, learning to cultivate happiness through gratitude and awareness is a lifelong process—so pick out a few exercises that you found the most worthwhile, and commit yourself to making them a permanent part of your daily life. You'll be grateful you did.